A TASTE OF CHICKEN SOUP

FOR THE

MOTHER'S SOUL

A TASTE OF CHICKEN SOUP

FOR THE

MOTHER'S SOUL

To Open the Hearts and Rekindle the Spirits of Mothers

Jack Canfield, Mark Victor Hansen
Jennifer Read Hawthorne
Marci Shimoff

Health Communications, Inc.
Deerfield Beach, Florida

www.bcibooks.com
www.chickensoup.com

All Those Years. Reprinted by permission of Alice Collins. ©1997 Alice Collins.

The Bobby Pins. Reprinted by permission of Linda Goodman. ©1997 Linda Goodman.

Moving Mountains. Reprinted by permission of Thomas Nelson Publishers. ©1997 Jim Stovall. Excerpted from You Don't Have to *Be Blind to See.* All rights reserved.

A Mother's Fight For a Special Child. Reprinted by permission of Tom Mulligan. ©1997 Tom Mulligan.

Tale of a Sports Mom. Reprinted by permission of Judy Bodmer. ©1997 Judy Bodmer.

The Stepmother. Reprinted by permission of Jennifer Graham. ©1997 Jennifer Graham.

Out of Our Hands. Reprinted by permission of Colleen Derrick Horning. ©1997 Colleen Derrick Horning.

When Mother Came to Tea. Reprinted by permission of Margie M. Coburn. ©1997 Margie M. Coburn.

Adopting a Dream. Reprinted by permission of Kathryn Lay. ©1997 Kathryn Lay.

Home Run for Mom. Reprinted by permission of John Morris. ©1997 John Morris.

John. Reprinted by permission of Muriel Cochrane. ©1997 Muriel Cochrane.

I Was Born for This Job. Reprinted by permission of Billie B. Chesney. ©1997 Billie B. Chesney.

Dinner Out. Reprinted by permission of Maryann Lee Jacobs. ©1997 Maryann Lee Jacobs.

Just Plain Wrong. Reprinted by permission of Gerald E. Thurston Jr. ©1997 Gerald E. Thurston Jr.

**Library of Congress Cataloging-in-Publication Data
is on file with the Library of Congress**

©2006 Jack Canfield, Mark Victor Hansen, Jennifer Read Hawthorne
and Marci Shimoff
ISBN 0-75730-510-5

Publisher: Health Communications, Inc.
3201 S.W. 15th Street
Deerfield Beach, FL 33442-8190

With love we dedicate this book to
our mothers, Ellen Taylor,
Una Hansen, Maureen Read
and Louise Shimoff, whose love and
guidance have been
the foundation for our lives.

We also dedicate this book to all mothers
everywhere, whose loving hands and hearts
have touched, healed and nurtured us all.

Contents

Introduction

This book is our gift to you, the mothers of the world. In writing this book, we wanted to honor mothers everywhere, but how can you thank a mother for the gift of life? As we read the thousands of stories that we considered for *Chicken Soup for the Mother's Soul,* and then excerpted for this "taste"ful shorter version, we were deeply moved by the depth of feeling people expressed for their mothers.

Many people talked about the sacrifices their mothers had made; others, how courageous their mothers were. Still others shared the inspiration and encouragement they had received from their mothers. But no theme was more widely expressed than that of the eternal nature of a mother's love.

So with love in our hearts, we offer you

this book. May you experience the miracles of love, joy and inspiration when you read it, and may it touch your heart and move your spirit.

Jack Canfield, Mark Victor Hansen, Jennifer
Read Hawthorne and Marci Shimoff

All Those Years

My friend Debbie's two daughters were in high school when she experienced severe flu-like symptoms. Debbie visited her family doctor, who told her the flu bug had passed her by. Instead, she had been touched by the "love bug" and was now pregnant.

The birth of Tommy, a healthy, beautiful son, was an event for celebration, and as time went by, it seemed as though every day brought another reason to celebrate the gift of Tommy's life. He was sweet, thoughtful, funloving and a joy to be around.

One day when Tommy was about five years old, he and Debbie were driving to the neighborhood mall. As is the way with children, out of nowhere, Tommy asked, "Mom, how old were you when I was born?"

"Thirty-six, Tommy. Why?" Debbie asked, wondering what his little mind was contemplating.

"What a shame!" Tommy responded.

"What do you mean?" Debbie inquired, more than a little puzzled. Looking at her with love-filled eyes, Tommy said, "Just think of all those years we didn't know each other."

Alice Collins

The Bobby Pins

When I was seven years old, I overheard my mother tell one of her friends that the following day was to be her 30th birthday. Two things occurred to me when I heard that: one, I had never before realized that my mother had a birthday; and two, I could not recall her ever getting a birthday present.

Well, I could do something about that. I went into my bedroom, opened my piggy bank and took out all the money that was inside: five nickels. That represented five weeks' worth of my allowance. Then I walked to the little store around the corner from my house, and I told the proprietor, Mr. Sawyer, that I wanted to buy a birthday present for my mother.

He showed me everything in his store that could be had for a quarter. There were several ceramic figurines. My mother would have loved those, but she already had a house full of them and I was the one who had to dust them once a week. They definitely would not do. There were also some small boxes of candy. My mother was diabetic, so I knew they would not be appropriate.

The last thing Mr. Sawyer showed me was a package of bobby pins. My mother had beautiful long black hair, and twice a week she washed and pincurled it. When she took the pincurls down the next day, she looked just like a movie star with those long, dark curls cascading around her shoulders. So I decided those bobby pins would be the perfect gift for my mother. I gave Mr. Sawyer my five nickels, and he gave me the bobby pins.

I took the bobby pins home and wrapped them in a colorful sheet from the Sunday comics (there was no money left for wrapping paper). The next morning, while my family was seated at the breakfast table, I walked up to my mother and handed her that package and said, "Happy birthday, Momma!"

My mother sat there for a moment in stunned silence. Then, with tears in her eyes, she tore at that comic-strip wrapping. By the time she got to the bobby pins, she was sobbing.

"I'm sorry, Momma!" I apologized. "I didn't mean to make you cry. I just wanted you to have a happy birthday."

"Oh, honey, I am happy!" she told me. And I looked into her eyes, and I could see that she was smiling through her tears. "Why, do you know that this is the first birthday present that I have ever received in my entire life?" she exclaimed.

Then she kissed me on the cheek and said, "Thank you, honey." And she turned to my sister and said, "Lookee here! Linda got me a birthday present!" And she turned to my brothers and said, "Lookee here! Linda got me a birthday present!" And she turned to my father and said, *"Lookee here! Linda got me a birthday present!"*

And then she went into the bathroom to wash her hair and pincurl it with her new bobby pins.

After she left the room, my father looked at me and said, "Linda, when I was growing up, back on the frontier (my daddy always called his childhood home in the mountains of Virginia *the frontier*), we didn't set much store by giving birthday presents to adults. That was something done just for small young 'uns. And your momma's family, they were so poor, they didn't even do that much. But seeing how happy you've made your momma today has made me rethink this whole birthday issue. What I'm trying to say, Linda, is I believe you have set a precedent here."

And I did set a precedent. After that, my mother was showered with birthday presents every year: from my sister, from my brothers, from my father and from me. And, of course, the older we children got, the more money we made, and the nicer presents she received. By the time I was 25, I had given her a stereo, a color television and a microwave oven (which she traded in for a vacuum cleaner).

For my mother's 50th birthday, my brothers and my sister and I pooled our resources and got her something spectacular: a ring set with a pearl surrounded by a cluster of diamonds. And when my oldest brother handed that ring to her at the party that was given in her honor, she opened up the velvet gift box and peered at the ring inside. Then she smiled and turned the box around so that her guests could see her special gift, and she said, "Don't I have wonderful children?" Then she passed the ring around the room, and it was thrilling to hear the collective sigh that rippled through that room as the ring was passed from hand to hand.

After the guests were gone, I stayed to help clean up. I was doing the dishes in the kitchen when I overheard a conversation between my mother and father in the next room. "Well, Pauline," my father said, "that's a mighty pretty ring you've got there. I reckon that's about the best birthday present you've ever had."

My own eyes filled with tears when I heard her reply. "Ted," she said softly, "that's a mighty pretty ring and that's a fact. But the best birthday present I ever got? Well, that was a package of bobby pins."

Linda Goodman

Moving Mountains

There were two warring tribes in the Andes, one that lived in the lowlands and the other high in the mountains. The mountain people invaded the lowlanders one day, and as part of their plundering of the people, they kidnapped a baby of one of the lowlander families and took the infant with them back up into the mountains.

The lowlanders didn't know how to climb the mountain. They didn't know any of the trails that the mountain people used, and they didn't know where to find the mountain people or how to track them in the steep terrain.

Even so, they sent out their best party of fighting men to climb the mountain and bring the baby home.

The men tried first one method of climbing and then another. They tried one trail and then another. After several days of effort, however, they had climbed only a couple of hundred feet.

Feeling hopeless and helpless, the lowlander men decided that the cause was lost, and they prepared to return to their village below.

As they were packing their gear for the descent, they saw the baby's mother walking toward them. They realized that she was coming down the mountain that they hadn't figured out how to climb.

And then they saw that she had the baby strapped to her back. *How could that be?*

One man greeted her and said, "We

couldn't climb this mountain. How did you do this when we, the strongest and most able men in the village, couldn't do it?"

She shrugged her shoulders and said, "It wasn't your baby."

Jim Stovall
Bits & Pieces

A Mother's Fight for a Special Child

No language can express the power and beauty and heroism of a mother's love.

EDWIN H. CHAPIN

Frank and Lee married in 1948 after serving in the Catholic church, he as a seminary student and she as a nun. When they started a family, Lee decided that she wanted six children. The first arrived in 1951, with five more following in the next 11 years. But by the time the fifth child, Tom, arrived, Lee was at the point where she wasn't sure she'd be able to care for another.

At six months, Tom still wasn't able to take spoon feedings or hold his head up. Lee felt that he was developing slowly in general. So she took him to the pediatrician, who told her that she was making a big deal over nothing.

"Lots of babies have trouble adjusting to spoon feedings," he told her. "This is normal."

"I think I know what's normal and not normal," she told him evenly. "I've had four others. There's something wrong."

So she took her baby to another doctor, who told her to wait a year to see if he would "grow out of it." So Lee waited— and watched.

Over the next year, Tom did manage to hold his head up, but in many other ways he got worse. He often refused to eat. Or he would eat only squash, until his skin turned an orange tinge. But the most worrisome development involved his violent outbursts. He would attack his older siblings while they watched television, or hit Lee from the back seat of the car while she tried to drive. Lee knew that temper tantrums are normal for a toddler, but the intensity of Tom's tantrums worried her.

When he was a year and a half, Lee made the rounds to the doctors and the specialists again. This time, no one told her Tom was normal. One doctor diagnosed PKU, a metabolic disease that can result in retardation. Another said it wasn't PKU, but brain damage at birth that had deprived the brain of oxygen. After a year, meeting this doctor and that doctor, Lee was told that Tom could never lead a normal life and should be institutionalized.

Lee was horrified. How could she send her child, only three years old, away to an institution, where the possibility of growing up healthy could be jeopardized forever? When Lee and Frank visited the institution the doctors suggested, all the children she saw there were seriously mentally disabled, many unable to communicate. Tom had problems, Lee decided, but this was not the place to send him.

Then a visiting nurse told Lee about a hospital in Ann Arbor that might be able to help Tom. The doctors and psychiatrists there concluded that he was mentally disabled and would never be able to finish high school. A social worker at the hospital suggested that Frank and Lee would find it a problem to raise a son with such limited capabilities, since they both had been to college.

"He'll never be anything more than a ditch digger," she said.

"So?" she retorted. "Let me tell you something. I don't care what he does for a living. I love all of my children. I don't love them based on their intelligence. It doesn't make me love Tom any less if he's not a genius."

But Tom exceeded the doctors' expectations. Reluctantly, the doctors agreed to let Tom attend a regular school. Although he experienced periods of difficulty, he not only graduated from high school, but also completed two-and-a-half years of college. Somewhere along the way, his mental disability was found to be emotionally based and was treated properly.

I'm glad Lee didn't give up on that child, because that child with the rough start in life was me. Today I'm on medication to control my emotional ups and downs. And when I look back on my early years, I thank God I had a mother who was so stubborn that she wouldn't listen to the doctors' pessimistic predictions for my bleak future. My mother loved me enough to listen to what her heart told her instead—that the best weapon in a fight for a child is a lot of faith and a lot of love.

Tom Mulligan

Tale of a Sports Mom

It's a chilly Saturday in May. I could be home sweeping cobwebs from the corners of the living room or curled up on the couch with a good mystery. Instead I'm sitting on a cold metal bench in the stands of a baseball park in Kirkland, Washington. An icy wind creeps through my heavy winter jacket. I blow on my hands, wishing I'd brought my woolen mittens.

"Mrs. Bodmer?" It's the coach my son Matthew admires so much that he gave up soda pop to impress him with his fitness.

"I'm starting your son today in right field. He's worked hard this year and I think he deserves the opportunity."

"Thanks," I say, feeling proud of my son who has given this man and this team everything he has. I know how badly he wants this. I'm glad his hard work is being rewarded.

Suddenly I'm nervous for him as the team members, in their white pinstriped uniforms, trot onto the field. I search for my son's number. It isn't there. Instead, Eddie, the most inexperienced player on the team, takes right field. I look again, unbelieving. How can that be?

I want to run over and ask the coach what's going on, but I know Matthew wouldn't like that. I've learned the proper etiquette for moms; talking to the coach is not acceptable unless he initiates it.

My son, gripping the chain-link fence in front of the dugout, is yelling encouragement to his teammates. I try to read his expression, but I know he, like most males, has learned to hide his feelings. My heart breaks because he has worked so hard and received so much disappointment. I don't understand what drives boys to put themselves through this.

"Atta boy, Eddie," yells the right-fielder's father, proud that his son is starting. I've seen this same man walk out of games in disgust when his son dropped a ball or made a bad throw. But for now, he is proud of his son, who is starting, while my son is on the bench.

By the fourth inning my fingers are stiff from the cold, and my feet are numb, but I don't care. Matthew has been called into the game. He stands, chooses a batting helmet, picks up a bat and struts out to the plate. I grip the metal seat. He takes a couple of practice swings. The pitcher looks like an adult. I wonder if anyone has checked his birth certificate.

Strike one. "Nice swing!" I yell. The next

pitch is a ball. "Good eye! Good eye!" Strike two. I pray. I cross my fingers. The pitcher winds up. I hold my breath. Strike three. My son's head hangs, and he slowly walks back to the dugout. I wish with all my heart I could help. But I know there's nothing I can do.

For eight years I've been sitting here. I've drunk gallons of terrible coffee, eaten tons of green hot dogs and salty popcorn. I've endured cold and heat, wind and rain.

Some people may wonder why a sane person would go through this. It's not because I want to fulfill my dream of excelling at sports through my kids. I also don't do this for the emotional highs. Oh, yes, I've had some. I've seen my two sons score winning goals in soccer, hit home runs in baseball, and spark come-from-behind wins in basketball. I've seen them make some incredible leaping catches in football. But mostly I've seen heartache.

I've waited with them for that phone

call telling them they'd made the team. The call that never came. I've watched coaches yell at them. I've watched them sit on the bench game after game. I've sat in emergency rooms as broken bones were set and swollen ankles x-rayed. I've sat here year after year, observing it all and wondering why.

The game ends. I stretch my legs and try to stomp life back into my frozen feet. The coach meets with the team. They yell some rallying cry and then descend on their parents. I notice Eddie's dad has a big grin and is slapping his son on the back. Matthew wants to get a hamburger. While I wait for him, the coach approaches me. I can't bring myself to look at him.

"Mrs. Bodmer, I want you to know that's a fine young man you have there."

I wait for him to explain why he broke my son's heart.

"When I told your son he could start, he thanked me and turned me down. He told me to let Eddie start, that it meant more to him."

I turn to watch my son stuffing his burger into his mouth. I realize then why I sit in the stands. Where else can I watch my son grow into a man?

Judy Bodmer

The Stepmother

Since our amicable divorce a few years before, Eric and I had maintained a comfortable relationship, remaining good friends. We had agreed on consistent parenting rules and visiting schedules, and our son, Charley, enjoyed a nice balance between our two homes. He seemed well-adjusted and happy.

So when I first met Eric's fiancée, the woman who was to become my son's stepmother, I was bound to be a little nervous. There was no doubt that Bonny would have an influence on my child's life. What I didn't appreciate at the time was the effect she would have on mine.

At that first meeting, I was struck by how opposite we were. Her clothes had a "dress for success" look, while I wore "rumpled nonchalance." She was attractive, composed and confident, while I was disheveled and nervous, prattling on about nothing. I was uncomfortable and suspicious, scrutinizing her every mannerism and inflection, sizing her up as my son's future parent. My prevailing thought was: "What will she do to my precious baby?"

Before this moment, I'd had various fantasies about who my "ex" might someday marry. One was of a wicked witch, a raving shrew from whom my son would run screaming. He would, of course, be running to me, his real mom, who would supply endless patience and wisdom, as only a true mother can.

Another fantasy was scarier. In this one she was the rock, his bridge over troubled water, where he could find solace from his nagging mom, who never understood him. Or even worse, she was the fun one, as in, "I can't come home tonight, Mom. Bonny got us the luxury suite for the Bulls championship."

Unfortunately, the latter of my fantasies wasn't a fantasy. This was a real person who was about to become my son's other mother, and all I could do was watch and wait.

Over time, I grew less wary and more natural around Bonny. She grew less coolly professional and more familiar around me. We found an easy way of working through the routines of pick-up and drop-off times, school conferences and soccer games.

Then one night my new husband and I invited Eric and Bonny to our house for coffee after a school conference. Charley, who loved to have us all together, was delighted. Over the course of the evening, tensions and pretensions melted away. Bonny and I let our walls down a bit and spoke more frankly. Instead of a complicated configuration of "ex's" and "steps," we were now just friends.

A few months later, the four of us got together to talk about Charley's grades. Instead of bringing her usual outlines, lists, data and literature—as if she were making a case before a committee—Bonny opened up and confessed her vulnerability. She talked about her insecurities and despair in dealing with Charley's adolescence. Was she demanding too much or asking too little? Was she pushing him or coddling him?

My heart went out to her. These were the same thoughts and fears that kept me up at night. She was thinking, feeling and behaving just like a mother—which is what she had become.

So Charley's second mom is neither an evil witch who would hurt my son, nor a fairy godmother who would steal him away. She's a woman who loves my little boy. She will worry over him, fight for him and protect him from harm.

I've gone from dreading Bonny's appearance to being grateful for her presence in Charley's life and mine. I welcome her unique perspective, her ideas—and even her lists. I was wrong to want to hold my child to my chest, like a toy. I didn't want to share. Maybe I was the first to love him, but that doesn't mean I should be the last. Now there's one more person in this world watching over him. And for that, I happily share the title Mom.

Jennifer Graham

Out of Our Hands

When the doorbell sounded that afternoon, I answered numbly. It was the worst
possible time for a repairman to come to
the house. I was nearly five months pregnant, and I had never been more emotionally on edge, waiting for the phone to ring.
In fact, it was the worst possible time for
our alarm system to malfunction, period.
Not only were our emotions on overload,
we didn't need another repair bill.

Our finances were shaky. I had morning
sickness from the get-go with my pregnancy,

and it became so bad I had to stop working, a loss of income we hadn't counted on quite yet. Although that was difficult, we were too excited to complain. We'd tried for a year and a half to have a baby and had even gone through the first phase of fertility testing, with no conclusive results. The next month, though, we got the call we'd dreamed about. I was pregnant!

The first trimester had been normal, except for the debilitating morning sickness, which I knew was temporary. I looked forward to each doctor visit, relishing the fact that we were learning more and more about our child. So when the doctor asked me if I wanted to have an optional blood test that would screen for spina bifida, among other things, in the growing fetus, I didn't hesitate to say yes.

When the results came back, our doctor had called immediately. In a professional yet concerned voice, he said that the test numbers were so low they were off the charts. Instead of suggesting spina bifida, the blood count suggested Down's syndrome.

The doctor immediately scheduled an amniocentesis. Even though my husband, Rob, and I were apprehensive, that day was also a thrill. The technician also used an ultrasound, so for the first time we got to see the baby move. It suddenly seemed all so real to me. We were really going to be parents, and the little person was a boy! Something cataclysmic couldn't really be wrong with him—could it?

Reality set in when we were told it would take two weeks for the results to come back. We were counseled that all the waiting for results was pushing us toward the end limit for a safe pregnancy termination. However, whatever the diagnosis, we didn't feel that was an option for us.

The wait was on. Never have I known two weeks to seem so endless. I tried to involve myself, to think about other things, but those words "off the charts" kept replaying in my mind. It didn't help when our home's built-in alarm system would blare for no reason when we least expected it. Rob, of course, went to work every day. I felt alone and helpless.

Finally the day arrived when we were supposed to get the answer. I'll never forget how nervous I was, at home all morning by myself, waiting for the phone to ring. It was silent. By noon I couldn't stand it any more. I called in, but the nurse said there were still no results.

Morning turned to afternoon. When the doorbell rang, I just about flew out of my skin. On automatic pilot, I let the repairman in, showed him the alarm system, and quickly left. Overwhelmed, my only thoughts about his arrival were a combination of, "This is gonna really cost us!" and, "Could there be any worse timing?" The faith that I'd been taught in "God's perfect timing" was beginning to show serious signs of wear and tear.

About two hours later, the nurse called. As I recall what she said, it almost started off like a bad joke: There was good news and bad news.

The good news was that our son did not have Down's syndrome. The bad news was that he did have two chromosomes that were joined. She explained that if either Rob or I had the same condition, our son should be okay. However, if neither of us had it, that meant there was something missing in the makeup of our baby's genes.

"Something missing?" I tried not to screech. "Like what? What does that mean?"

"I'm sorry, Mrs. Horning, there is no way we can tell what's wrong with him until he's born. Now, the best thing is for you and your husband to come in right away for a blood test."

"Right away? We can find out today?"

"We can do the test today. We'll have the results in five days."

Five days?

That's when I lost control. I became hysterical. I don't remember ever screaming or crying like that in all of my 34 years of life. It felt as if someone had punched me in the stomach, and I had regained my breath long enough to have it done again.

I remember calling Rob at work, still hysterical.

"Colleen, honey, listen to me. I want you to go next door to the neighbor's house, okay? Colleen? I'll leave as soon as I can, but I don't want you to stay there alone."

But his words and frantic urgings for me to get help couldn't cut through the panic that had overtaken me. I let the phone drop into the cradle.

As I sat gasping by the phone, I realized that the repairman was still working in the front room. I couldn't believe he had heard all of this. Deeply chagrined, I felt I had to apologize. I walked around the corner, still weeping.

He was standing in the doorway, as if he were waiting for me. Before I could say anything, he guided me to a chair. "Sit down," he instructed. "Just sit down and catch your breath."

The specific instructions and the gentle tone caught me off guard. As I sat and breathed, I felt myself calming down.

This stranger sat down right across from me. In a quiet voice, he told me how he and his wife had lost their first child. The baby had been born dead because they didn't realize his wife had developed diabetes during her pregnancy.

He went on to explain how hard it was for them to accept this, but they finally had to give it up and admit it was something that was beyond their control.

He looked at me and said, "I understand how badly your heart is hurting right now. But there's nothing you can do but have faith, and realize what's happening with your baby is out of your control. The more you try to take it back, to try to keep control of the baby, of the tests, the worse your inability to change anything is going to tear at you."

He took my hand and told me their second child was born a few months ago. This time there were no problems. He and his wife were blessed with a healthy little girl.

He told me he still thinks about his first child, who was a little boy, but for whatever reason, that wasn't meant to be. He asked me to please try to keep faith about my baby, and that he felt our situation would turn out all right.

Then, as quietly as he told me his story, he got up and walked to the front door. He turned around and told me that he was finished, the alarm was fixed.

He had helped me in a way that no one else could have—what could I possibly say? All that came out was a meek thank-you.

Then I remembered I hadn't paid him.

He smiled and said I didn't owe him anything. All he asked was for me to keep faith.

The timing, as it turned out, was perfect.

Colleen Derrick Horning

[EDITOR'S NOTE: *Colleen and Rob's son was born four months later. He weighed 9 pounds, 2½ ounces, and is the picture of health.*]

When Mother Came to Tea

I had no idea she would be there. My apologies for her absence had been well-rehearsed.

When my high school home economics teacher announced that we would be having a formal mother-daughter tea, I felt certain I would not be serving my mother at this special event.

So I will never forget walking into the gaily decorated gym—and there she was! As I looked at her, sitting calmly and smiling, I imagined all the arrangements this remarkable woman must have had to make to be able to be with me for that one hour.

Who was looking after Granny? She was bedridden following a stroke, and Mom had to do everything for her.

My three little sisters would be home from school before Mom got there. Who would greet them and look at their papers?

How did she get here? We didn't own a car, and she couldn't afford a taxi. It was a long walk to get the bus, plus at least five more blocks to the school.

And the pretty dress she was wearing, red with tiny white flowers, was just right for the tea. It brought out the silver beginning to show in her dark hair. There was no money for extra clothes, and I knew she had gone into debt again at our coal company store to have it.

I was so proud! I served her tea with a happy, thankful heart, and introduced her boldly to the group when our turn came. I sat with my mother that day, just like the rest of the class, and that was very important to me. The look of love in her eyes told me she understood.

I have never forgotten. One of the promises I made to myself and to my children, as young mothers make promises, was that I would always be there for them. That promise is difficult to keep in today's busy world. But I have an example before me that puts any lame excuses to rest. I just recall again when Mother came to tea.

Margie M. Coburn

Adopting a Dream

Michael or Michelle.

Before Richard and I married, we agreed that this would be the name of our first child. We had it all planned.

Two years later, Richard walked across the stage to receive his college diploma. It was time to make our dream come true for a family.

For the next two years, we prayed that I would get pregnant. Yet month after month was filled with disappointment, until one day in the spring of 1985, I was so sure I was pregnant that I made an appointment to see the doctor.

With a smile, he said, "You're pregnant."

I wanted to dance around the room. My due date was set for the first week of November, "around the third," my doctor said.

The next six weeks were filled with preparations. We did everything but take out an ad in the newspaper. Richard began preparing the room that would be the nursery.

We tried to imagine what our son or daughter would be like. My thoughts were consumed with the child growing inside me.

"I'm concerned that we haven't heard a heartbeat," my doctor told me on my third visit.

A half-hour later, I cried in his office when he explained that a blood test showed no sign of my ever having been pregnant.

"A false pregnancy," he said. "Your mind wanted it so badly, your body believed it."

Little Michael or Michelle didn't exist. There was no baby to mourn, yet we grieved.

So began nearly a decade of infertility tests and watching enviously as our friends and siblings had babies. My heart ached as I forced smiles when they talked of their children.

More pregnancy tests. More pacing and praying. Negative. They were always the same. The dream died again and again.

We plunged into our work—Richard into his teaching and I into my writing. Yet our desire for a child was strong, and in 1992 we attended an adoption orientation class.

I looked around the crowded room of nervous couples. Could our dream really come true?

I was afraid to hope.

"This is our chance," Richard whispered.

We began our required parenting classes. Every Monday evening for 10 weeks we listened, role-played, and discussed the joys and trials of parenting these children who needed new homes.

With all the work came the joy of preparation. How long before our child arrived? Would he or she come with a broken heart and spirit? How long would it take to bond with our child, and he with us? Would our child be anything like the one I'd imagined so long ago?

Together Richard and I prepared our extra bedroom. Would it be a nursery or child's room? There were so many plans to make, yet so little information to help us. Lovingly I placed bottles of lotion and powders beside bibs and books, inside dresser drawers.

Often, I sat on the floor in the yellow and white room and dreamed of the child who would sleep and play there. I bought a few toys and stuffed animals. They waited quietly for small hands to hold them.

Then, on November 3, 1993, the phone rang and our lives changed.

"Kathy, is there something you've been wanting for Christmas?" our caseworker asked.

I could almost hear her smiling. I clutched the phone and whispered, "Yes."

"Well, we've got some good news."

Then she told me about an eight-month-old girl. A baby girl! Would I awake and find it just another dream?

"Her name is Theresa Michelle. But her foster parents call her Michelle," I was told.

I was stunned. Michelle. Eight years ago, we'd dreamed of our Michelle. Then it hit me. It was November 3. If I had had that child in November of 1985, "around the third," my doctor had said, he or she would be eight years old. How wonderful God was to us, how our prayers had been answered!

I tried to imagine what it would be like holding this child.

Within two weeks, we began our three days of visitation. I looked into my daughter's face. She smiled and held her arms out. I held her and breathed in the scent of baby powder and milk, as sweet smelling as a garden of roses.

Our Michelle had arrived.

On November 23, she came to live in our home and hearts. Every day our love for her grows. Nearly four years old now, she loves to hear the story of her adoption, of how we waited and longed for her.

Hopes and dreams don't have to die. We watched ours come back to life and call us Mama and Daddy.

Kathryn Lay

Home Run for Mom

*That which the fountain sends forth
returns again to the fountain.*
HENRY WADSWORTH LONGFELLOW

When my five-year professional baseball career with the St. Louis Cardinals came to an end in 1990, I prayed for the chance to play closer to New York. My mother, Grace, had been diagnosed with breast cancer. She was living on Long Island, and I wanted to spend more time with her. My wish came true when I signed with the Philadelphia Phillies for the 1991 season.

Philadelphia was just three short hours from her home.

As the 1991 baseball season progressed, Mom's condition took a turn for the worse. The cancer was spreading, and she couldn't hold on for much longer. My fiancée and I even got married four months earlier than planned so Mom could attend.

My performance was also taking a turn for the worse. After the All-Star break, my playing time was reduced, and the few games I played were anything but impressive. Over the next six weeks, I went hitless in 18 consecutive at bats. This was a long slump, and I felt everything from self-pity to loneliness.

My downturn came to an end in the September 1 game against the Atlanta Braves. Playing in Philadelphia on a gorgeous Sunday afternoon, I entered the game as a leadoff pinch-hitter in the bottom of the tenth. With the score tied 4–4, I batted against one of the hardest-throwing pitchers in the league, Mark Wohlers. I just wanted to do anything to get on base so that we could win the game.

I took the first two pitches as the count reached one ball and one strike. Then I fouled off the next two pitches on fastballs that were clocked in excess of 95 mph! After those two healthy cuts, I finally felt a competitive spirit rise up inside me again.

With the count two balls and two strikes, I stepped out of the box and mentally prepared myself for the hardest pitch my adversary could possibly throw, determined not to be late again. The fastball was delivered over the inside corner, and the ball jumped off my bat with a thunderous crack usually reserved for superstar home-run hitters.

Right-fielder David Justice went back to the wall and watched the ball sail over the fence for a game-winning home run. Mobbed by my teammates at home plate, I could feel my heart pumping so fast I thought it was going to come crashing through my jersey. What a feeling!

Two weeks later, I visited Mom, eager to show her a videotape of the home run. But when I walked into her room, I was shocked to see the physical condition of my dear mother. I knew that this would probably be the last visit I would ever have with her.

We were both watching the tape for the first time, so I didn't anticipate the commentator's story that would unfold. After I hit the home run, the announcer, Harry Kalas, explained that it had been six long weeks since my last hit. Mom and I held hands and listened to Kalas continue. "John Morris has really struggled the second half of this season, and this couldn't have happened to a nicer guy." I could feel the tears building up inside the two of us, as he showed a slow motion replay of my dramatic home run. As the pitcher wound up, Kalas uttered the sweetest words my mom had ever heard. "John's mom has been quite ill for some time," and as the ball connected with the bat, he finished, "and this one was probably for his mom."

Mom and I broke down. She hugged me as tightly as she could and whispered into my ear, "I love you son, and I'm very proud of you. I'm going to miss you very much."

The season was ending the last weekend of September when I received a call that Mom was not expected to make it through the weekend. That Sunday afternoon, the last out of the season was recorded, and on Monday morning she passed away with me at her bedside. It was as if she knew the season was complete, and that it was all right to let go.

John Morris

John

I saw him first in April
When they said, "You have a boy,"
I waited long to hear these words
So he became my joy.

And every time his birthday came
I saw him growing tall,
And then he started off to school
In just no time at all.

It seemed I only turned around
And he was in his teens,

He went around in funny hats
And had his favorite jeans.

Then track and football filled his life,
His high school days were fun,
And in his private treasure box
Went medals that he'd won.

And often when he came back home
From being on a date,
He'd whisper at my bedroom door,
"Mom, are you still awake?"

Then we would talk a little while
Before he went to bed,
And I would often breathe a prayer,
"God bless my son," I said.

I saw him last in April
When he said, "Mom, don't you worry,
I'm leaving for Vietnam—
We'll win this in a hurry."

But he will nevermore be back,
My heart still seems to break,
I'll never hear him whisper now,
"Mom, are you still awake?"

Yet I thank God for every joy
For all the love and fun,
And locked in my heart's treasure box
Are memories of my son.

Muriel Cochrane

I Was Born for This Job

If I'd known grandchildren were going to be so much fun, I'd have had them first.

ANONYMOUS

As a novice grandma, I eagerly looked forward to the first time I'd hear, "Mom, can you keep the baby a couple of days?" My response? "I'm ready! How soon can you get here?"

The calendar was cleared of bridge clubs and tennis matches. The crib was set up in the guest room, and friends were put on alert that I would be holding open house for the debut of our little princess. This cherub, a living, breathing angel, was to be all mine for two-and-a-half days. Talk about your dividends!

And talk about your responsibility! Instinct told me that taking care of my child's child was going to be a whole different diaper pail. (Diaper pail—what we Neanderthals put dirty cloth diapers in before laundering them. Yes, we laundered them.) I invested in a fresh copy of Dr. Spock. I was actually worried that if I didn't do a good job at this baby-sitting routine, they wouldn't let me do it again.

The new parents arrived with a two-week supply of clothes, enough disposable diapers to soak up the Mississippi River, an entire zoo of stuffed animals, stroller, car seat, an itinerary of their hourly whereabouts for the next two days, the phone number of their pediatrician (60 miles away), their personal copy of Dr. Spock (with notes in the margins), and six pages of instructions. They left the collie at home.

The instructions included a 6:30 A.M. to 7:30 P.M. feeding/sleeping schedule. The baby must have read it because she followed it to the letter, even though there was a notation that "these times are estimates." That darling baby had been in this world barely four months, and she had four people ready to do her bidding, willing to keep a record of said bidding and call it a schedule. Our son's parting remarks were classic father-of-first-child edicts.

"Now, Mom, let her cry sometimes." (What kind of sadist did I raise here?!)

"You don't have to pick her up every time she opens her eyes." (I've waited four months to pick this child up whenever I want!)

"It's a matter of discipline, you know, and it must start early." (This from a boy who at 15 needed 45 logical reasons he couldn't hitchhike 300 miles to a high school basketball tournament.)

I was up at 5:30 that first day. She made me sit and watch her breathe until 6:45. Grandpa went to work and didn't get to stay home and watch her breathe. For some reason he didn't think that a major sacrifice.

My beautiful granddaughter and I had a wonderful day. I dressed her in her finest and we danced around the living room and strolled up and down the block. She responded beautifully for all the potential grandmothers who dropped by, then slept most of the afternoon, no doubt worn out from being adorable. She continued to follow the schedule. What a good baby!

What a joyful experience—pleasuring in that first grandchild. As I held her I looked into her father's baby eyes again. They crinkled and sparkled with each toothless giggle. I nuzzled the soft cheeks and inhaled the sweet baby-fresh scent, long

forgotten and greatly missed. This grandchild had added a dimension to life impos-
sible to measure or explain. And all her
father's sins, from colic to wrecking the
family car, were forgiven.

The second night, Baby decided to see
how quickly Grandma could get to her crib
when she called. Grandma hit the floor
running each time. Baby called at 1:00,
hungry. I fed her. She called at 2:30, wanting to smile and play. At 4:00 she was
chewing her fist. I fed her. At 5:00 what I
had fed her at 4:00 reappeared all over her
and the crib. We both slept through her
6:30 feeding. I don't think she missed it.

She remained happy and content for the
rest of our time together, glorying in her
star status, until five minutes before her
parents walked in the front door. At that
moment she woke up screaming, for no
reason I could comprehend other than she
had forgotten the schedule. They found
me, her parents did, hair stringing, shirttail

out, walking the floor and crooning. Her mother grabbed my precious from me. Immediately the crying stopped. I never convinced them that Baby hadn't done that for two days.

But I had passed my maiden grandbaby-sitting test, and they did let me do it again. And again. And again. And so did our other children, so by the time I was rocking my seventh baby grand, my beginner's luck had seasoned to old pro status.

It's been 20 years since I heard the first, "Mom, can you . . .?" and my response is still, "I'm ready. How soon can you get here?"

Billie B. Chesney

Dinner Out

We went to a little cafe
    just off the campus
    to have a quiet dinner together,
the college students there
    eating, discussing deep philosophical
    issues.

You sat at our table
    looking suave and debonair in jeans
    and turtleneck,
    your tousled hair shining,
    your eyes sparkling, full of mischief.

And you worked your charms
    on me and everyone around.

The waitress doted on you,
    your cup always filled
"An extra napkin? Certainly!"
"More crackers for your soup? Of course!"
You flirted notoriously with her
    and with the hostess as well,
    flashing seductive grins at them,
    inviting them to talk,
    eating only the fringes of your meal.
Twice you left our table
    to walk around
    and spread your charms elsewhere,
    stopping at a table or two,
    grinning broadly, flirtatiously,
    soliciting conversation.
I watched you captivate their hearts
    and knew you had taken mine,
    as I sat quietly observing.

Finally, folding my dinner napkin patiently
    and placing it beside my finished plate,
I knew it was time to go,
and walking up to you I said,
    "Let's say good-bye."

And picking you up, I placed you
    in your stroller,
    and as we left,
you waved profusely at everyone,
after your first dinner out with Grandma,
    when you were only two.

Maryann Lee Jacob

Just Plain Wrong

To say my mother was plain is neither criticism nor complaint. She was, in fact, simply one of those women whom people didn't notice. The world is full of the proverbial "plain Jane" types.

Born into a painfully long line of alcoholics, my mother decided at the age of 17 to leave St. Louis because, as she put it, "I couldn't take another minute of the fighting and drinking and craziness." She moved in with her California cousin and his family to begin a new life. That was in 1959.

In 1960, she married my father—a Navy man—and over the next four years they had Tammy, Tina and me, Jerry. My parents bought a small, plain house in Orange County in 1967. In 1975, having both given it their best, my parents divorced. I was 12.

Maybe it was because of the enormous change a divorce brings, I don't know— but I suddenly noticed my mother more as a person than a parent. I started noticing her face with its unstartling features. Her eyes had great dark circles about them, and her shape had suffered the fate of the birthing process and its aftermath. Men did not notice my single mother. They never seemed to notice those flaming eyes that I'd begun to take note of as time passed.

As single mothers often have to do, mine took a second job at night delivering racing forms to liquor stores. She used to promise me a chocolate-dipped cone from Foster's Freeze if I'd just ride along with her, saying it was the only time she got to see me anymore. She would take stacks of forms into the liquor stores, barely getting a grunt out of the men behind the counters. My mother seemed invisible to men.

As I grew into a young man, I became silently bitter about people's general disinterest in my mother. I knew the lethal wit she wielded and the immense knowledge she'd acquired from having been an insatiable reader. It was all right there in those eyes. It wasn't a critical observation typical of teenagers when it comes to their parents. I simply noticed that my mother's silently heroic life was passing by unmarked, unappreciated. It pained me.

On February 19th, 1986, I got a phone call in the middle of my shift at a wholesale warehouse. It was my mother, with the news that the cold she'd been trying to shake for two months was due to a tumor in her left lung that had "trapped" the cold inside. A week later a surgeon opened her up, noticed that the tumor had wrapped around her aorta in an upward spiral toward her heart, and promptly closed her chest back up. He spoke at length of chemotherapy and radiation, but his eyes gave us the truth.

My plain mother fought that tumor like a warrior, and no one seemed to notice. She withstood the effects of radiation on her voice box and on her abilities to swallow and even breathe. In no plain fashion, she faced the nightmare of chemotherapy, even buying a screaming red wig to try to lighten the family up about the whole thing. It didn't work. She vowed to "beat this beast," until she lost consciousness on February 2, 1987, and passed away with her three children holding both hands and stroking those plain, unstartling cheeks. It angered me.

I was enraged at the world for not having noticed her. I noticed her. I watched the struggle and the loneliness take their toll on her. How could they fail to see that this physically uninspiring woman was, in fact, a gorgeous human being? I was furious until the funeral.

People I didn't know began pouring into the plain, little chapel where my mother was to be noticed for the last time. Coworkers from jobs two decades before came in, telling me that the last time they saw me I was in diapers. Friends I never knew about from the job she'd had until she was too sick to work flooded in, hugging my sisters and me. Even her racing form boss from eight years earlier came, shook my hand, and told me that my plain mother was "just about the kindest woman I ever knew."

I'd started noticing my mother as a person at 12, and I felt her life plain. I looked out at the standing-room-only chapel filled with good people who had noticed my mother, and who had judged her as anything but plain. She had made her mark on their lives, and I'd never noticed.

It never felt so good to be so wrong. They'd noticed all along, and I wasn't angry anymore.

Gerald E. Thurston Jr.

More Chicken Soup?

We enjoy hearing your reactions to the stories in *Chicken Soup for the Soul* books. Please let us know what your favorite stories were and how they affected you.

Many of the stories and poems you enjoy in *Chicken Soup for the Soul* books are submitted by readers like you who had read earlier *Chicken Soup for the Soul* selections.

We invite you to contribute a story to one of these future volumes.

Stories may be up to 1,200 words and

must uplift or inspire. To obtain a copy of
our submission guidelines and a listing of
upcoming *Chicken Soup* books, please write,
fax or check our Web sites.

Chicken Soup for the Soul
P.O. Box 30880
Santa Barbara, CA 93130
Fax: 805-563-2945
Web sites: *www.chickensoup.com*

Supporting Mothers and Children

In the spirit of supporting mothers and children everywhere, the publisher and coauthors proceeds from the sale of the original *Chicken Soup for the Mother's Soul* are donated to the Save the Children Federation, Inc.

Save the Children, a nonprofit organization, is dedicated to making lasting, positive changes in the lives of disadvantaged children in the United States and throughout the world. For 65 years, Save the Children has been working with families and communities in 40 nations, developing and managing programs in health, education, economic opportunity and emergency relief. Its programs reach more than 1.5 million children and their families in Africa, Asia, Europe, Latin America, the Middle East and the United States.

In 1997, Save the Children launched a new initiative in the United States: Save the Children U.S. will focus on the issue of keeping kids safe and maximizing their potential during out-of-school time. Save the Children U.S. will provide children with access to caring adults, secure places and structured activities during their after school hours, when 44 percent of American children are unsupervised.

Save the Children Federation, Inc.
54 Wilton Road
P.O. Box 950
Westport, CT 06880
Phone: 800-243-5075

Who Is Jack Canfield?

Jack Canfield is one of America's leading experts in the development of human potential and personal effectiveness. He is both a dynamic, entertaining speaker and a highly sought-after trainer. Jack has a wonderful ability to inform and inspire audiences toward increased levels of self-esteem and peak performance.

In addition to the *Chicken Soup for the Soul* series, Jack has coauthored numerous books, including *The Success Principles, How to Get From Where You Are to Where You Want to*

Be with Janet Switzer, *The Aladdin Factor* with Mark Victor Hansen, *100 Ways to Build Self-Concept in the Classroom* with Harold C. Wells, *Heart at Work* with Jacqueline Miller and *The Power of Focus* with Les Hewitt and Mark Victor Hansen.

Jack is regularly seen on television shows such as *Good Morning America, 20/20* and *NBC Nightly News.* For further information about Jack's books, tapes and training programs, or to schedule him for a presentation, please contact:

Self-Esteem Seminars
P.O. Box 30880
Santa Barbara, CA 93130
Phone: 805-563-2935 • Fax: 805-563-2945
Web site: *www.chickensoup.com*

Who Is Mark Victor Hansen?

In the area of human potential, no one is better known and more respected than Mark Victor Hansen. For more than thirty years, Mark has focused solely on helping people from all walks of life reshape their personal vision of what's possible. .

He is a sought-after keynote speaker, bestselling author and marketing maven. Mark is a prolific writer with many best-selling books such as *The One Minute Millionaire, The Power of Focus, The Aladdin Factor* and *Dare to Win,* in addition to the

Chicken Soup for the Soul series.

As a passionate philanthropist and humanitarian, he has been the recipient of numerous awards that honor his entrepreneurial spirit, philanthropic heart and business acumen for his extraordinary life achievements, which stand as a powerful example that the free enterprise system still offers opportunity to all.

Mark Victor Hansen & Associates, Inc.
P.O. Box 7665
Newport Beach, CA 92658
Phone: 949-764-2640 • Fax: 949-722-6912
Web site: *www.markvictorhansen.com*

Who Is Jennifer Read Hawthorne?

Jennifer Read Hawthorne is coauthor of the #1 *New York Times* bestseller *Chicken Soup for the Woman's Soul.* She also delivers *Chicken Soup for the Soul* presentations nationwide, sharing inspirational stories of love and hope, courage and dreams.

As a Peace Corps volunteer in West Africa teaching English, Jennifer discovered the universality of stories to teach, move, uplift and connect people.

Jennifer is cofounder of The Esteem

Group, a company specializing in self-esteem and inspirational programs for women. As a professional speaker she has spoken to thousands of people around the world about personal growth, self-development and professional success.

Jennifer graduated from Louisiana State University with a degree in journalism, and lives in Fairfield, Iowa, with her family.

If you would like to schedule Jennifer for a *Chicken Soup for the Soul* keynote address or seminar, you may contact her at:

Jennifer Hawthorne Inc.
1105 South D Street
Fairfield, IA 52556
Phone: 515-472-7136 • Fax: 515-469-6908

Who Is Marci Shimoff?

Marci Shimoff is coauthor of the #1 *New York Times* bestseller *Chicken Soup for the Woman's Soul,* and a professional speaker and trainer who inspires people to grow personally and professionally.

She gives seminars on self-esteem, stress management, communication skills and peak performance. In the last few years, she has specialized in delivering *Chicken Soup for the Soul* keynote addresses.

Marci is cofounder and president of The Esteem Group, a company that offers self-esteem and inspirational programs for women.

Marci earned her MBA from UCLA and has an advanced certificate as a stress-management consultant. Of all the projects Marci has worked on in her career, none have been as fulfilling as creating *Chicken Soup for the Soul* books.

If you would like to schedule Marci for a *Chicken Soup for the Soul* keynote address or seminar, you can reach her at:

The Esteem Group
191 Bayview Drive
San Rafael, CA 94901
Phone: 415-789-1300 • Fax: 415-789-1309

Contributors

Judy Bodmer watched her sons, who are now in college, play sports for over 10 years in Kirkland, Washington. She works as a library assistant at Lake Forest Park and teaches creative writing at Lake Washington Technical College. Along with her husband, Larry, she volunteers her time working with engaged and married couples through her church.

Billie B. Chesney is a native of Kansas. She is a grandmother of five, a Bible study leader and a freelance writer. Her essays, short stories and reminiscences have won several awards and have been published in Good Old Days, Cappers and One of a Kind magazines. A theme book soon to be published by Reminisce magazine will include some of her work. Billie and her husband, Dale, live in Kingsport, Tennessee.

Margie Coburn retired recently from her local hospital after 25 years. Her freelance writings are mostly inspirational or reflective of her interesting, happy life experiences. She enjoys church work, public speaking and being a volunteer historical site tour guide. She lives at 106 Azalea St., Greenville, NC 27834 or call 919-752-3219.

Muriel Cochrane and her husband are in their 80s. They lost their son, John in 1966 during the Vietnam War. They have four lovely daughters, 14 grandchildren and 25 great-grandchildren. Muriel has written several poems over the years dealing with home, family and friendships.

Alice Collins, wife, mother, and grandmother defrosts chicken, has hot flashes, misplaces her glasses and celebrates family life in her columns and books, or when speaking in front of audiences. She can be reached next to the overflowing hamper in Oak Lawn, Illinois, at 708-422-7568.

Linda Goodman has shared her stories with audiences throughout the country. She was the 1995 recipient of the Excellency in Storytelling Award presented by Connecticut's Storytelling Institute. Her tape, Jesse and Other Stories, and her short-story collection, Daughters of the Appalachians, have received glowing reviews. You can reach Linda at 978-562-9575.

Jennifer Graham lives in Naperville, Illinois, with her husband, Bob, and their two children, Charley and Katherine. Jennifer's colorful family provides endless material for her freelance writing. She can be reached at 630-717-6788.

Colleen Derrick Horning is a segment producer for WFAA-TV's Good Morning Texas, which airs live daily on ABC in Dallas, Texas. She especially enjoys producing the "Mom" segments. Her husband, Rob, also works at WFAA-TV. They've been married for six years and their combined family includes Nicholas, 16, and Sterling, 4. Colleen, as any writing mother would do, logs Sterling's amazing daily quotes. His latest: "Lucy, I'm home!"

Maryann Lee Jacob is a psychology teacher at Stevens High School in Rapid City, South Dakota. She has several poems published in South Dakota's Prairie Winds.

She also has a college grammar book published entitled Fundamentals of English. She has five children and can be reached at 3304 Idlewild Court, Rapid City, SD or call 605-341-2843.

Kathryn Lay is a freelance writer and author living in Bedord, Texas, with her husband, Richard, and their daughter. Her writing includes personal experiences and inspirational pieces as well as children's fiction. She can be reached at 817-285-0166.

John Morris is a motivational speaker and writer who uses his major league baseball experiences—including playing in the World Series—as metaphors to illustrate techniques and attitudes needed for business and personal success. John lives with his wife, Linda, and two cats in St. Petersburg, Florida. You can reach him at 813-345-2722.

Tom Mulligan is a freelance writer living in North Michigan. He writes articles, essays and fiction. He can be contacted for writing assignments at 8427 E. Au Sable Rd., St. Helen, MI 48656.

Gerald E. Thurston Jr. is the drug prevention coordinator for a school district in Visalia, California. He is also pursuing a master's degree in interpersonal communication. He writes creatively as a hobby and is available to present workshops on organizational and interpersonal communication. He can be reached at 209-625-8805.